Élan Vital

A Chapbook of Oriental Poetry and *Sumi-e* Painting

Élan Vital

A Chapbook of Oriental Poetry and *Sumi-e* Painting

by
Mary Elizabeth Rodning
Charles Bernard Rodning

CHARLES E. TUTTLE COMPANY
Rutland, Vermont & Tokyo, Japan

*Published by the Charles E. Tuttle Company, Inc., of Rutland, Vermont &
Tokyo, Japan, with editorial offices at 2-6 Suido 1-chome, Bunkyo-ku, Tokyo.
Copyright © 1988 by Charles Bernard Rodning. All rights reserved.
Library of Congress Catalog Card No. 88-50166
International Standard Book No. 0-8048-1539-9
First printing, 1988*

Printed in Japan

Contents

We dedicate
this chapbook to our children:
KAI JOHANNES, SOREN PIERS, and
CHRISTOPHER BERNARD RODNING

Élan Vital

Vita Brevis, Ars Longa

Preface

Henri Louis Bergson (1859–1941), a Frenchman and "process" philosopher, published his most famous monograph *L'Evolution créatrice* [Creative Evolution] in 1907. He cogently argued that the entire evolutionary process should be interpreted as the endurance of an *élan vital* (vital impulse or force) that is continually developing and generating new forms of life and expression. He argued that evolution is creative, continuous, dynamic, and holistic.

Perhaps, at an aesthetic and artistic level, it is.

Mary Elizabeth Rodning
Charles Bernard Rodning

Acknowledgments

Grateful acknowledgment is made to the following publications in which some of the poems in this chapbook first appeared: *The Red Pagoda, Proof Rock, Orphic Lute, Dragonfly, Modern Haiku, Piedmont Literary Review*, and *Daring Poetry Quarterly*.

The excerpt on page 14 is from Sato Shozo, *The Art of Sumi-e, Appreciation, Techniques and Application*, Kodansha International Ltd., Tokyo, 1984.

Introduction

Fundamental to the creation of any artistic work, two interdependent instincts are operational. First, an instinct for expression, to communicate a view of life, to discover meaning, to contemplate the world and the universe. Second, an instinct for aesthetics, to secure pleasure, to experience beauty and truth. The consequences of an artist's product—the medium and technique, the theme and style— are determined not only by his technical ability, but also by his perception and interpretation of nature and human endeavor. Ideally, an artistic work would be an eclectic expression of life, of truth, of the universal, untrammeled and unfettered, it is hoped, by rules and conventions.

It is from this contemplation and expression that the extreme pleasure afforded by art derives, a pleasure that

results from the pursuit of, and experiencing of, reality. Thus, "artistic" in this context may mean more or less the same as "religious"; when an artist produces a work, his awareness expands in every direction and is amplified, assimilating the vast and profound truth of life in a way impossible in ordinary, everyday activity. The act of artistic expression thus becomes a statement of the universal, and as such is an act of worship in the deepest sense. It is a characteristic of art that the contemplation of life that is its prime objective also carries with it the elevation and joy of a profound religious experience— the joy that arises with the growth of truth in the mind of the artist. (Sato, 1984)

Art, such as poetry and painting, should act as an aesthetic and spiritual prod to the receptive viewer, *prepared* to perceive. The stimuli to enlightenment are present constantly, if only we have "eyes to see and ears to hear" them, so that we grasp and apply them to our own existence. Su Shih of the Sung Dynasty (960–1297 C.E.)

commenting upon the work of the artist Wang Wei (698–759 C.E.) observed the close relationship between poetry and painting:

> Reading his poems, one sees pictures;
> looking at his pictures, one senses poetry.
>
> Picturesque poems—lyrical paintings.

The transmission of the essence and meaning of an artistic work demands much of an artist. It requires a keen observation of nature, a sensitive rendition of detail, an elegant arrangement of elements, a nuance and subtlety of hue and tone. It requires intense daily practice, with conscientious copying and adopting of selected past masters to produce a reservoir of knowledge and skill, which, at a spirited moment, may raise his intuitive performance to an incredible height, combining callowness and discipline.

Ideas are poetic, and a key element of Oriental poetry and painting is to express those ideas in brush and ink. The choice of

expressive mode is with the artist: write a poem and express it calligraphically; draw a wordless painting with poetic feeling; write a poem and brush it over a picture. All that the artist has learned from the past in terms of styles and traditions, all that is perceived in natural environments, and all that is experienced in life, is focused and expressed with a brush tip, and left as traces of ink.

With the creation of the Oriental poetry and *sumi-e* paintings within this volume, the artist and author have attempted to convey their interpretation of the variety, beauty, and novelty of nature and human endeavor. The artist and author would argue that the *puissance* of their work lies not only in what is explicitly conveyed, but what is implicit as a consequence of interpretation and extrapolation by the viewer. The latter must be receptive and interactive to achieve enlightenment and self-actualization. It would be our hope that through this work, the viewer also would become one with nature, as exemplified by the Japanese term *kenshō* ("contemplation," or to "turn a Zen light on things"), as part of the process of their personal development toward complete insight and enlightenment. We wish for the viewer enrichment and ennoblement. The conveyance of this wish and the creation of this chapbook are our karma.

The Poems

a split-rail fence
   ten thousand cawing crows —
spring returning

old farmer
     yoking a water buffalo
rice fields

misty dawn —
 sunrise streaking thru the pine
fog burning away

spring rains
  winter melting into the lowlands —
swollen cinnamon river

waning bitter winds —
  yellow crocus thru the snow —
early morning thaw

a downy woodpecker
chiseling a rotting gnarled oak
spring nest

a blackbird
  alighting a willow branch
rippling pond

Summer 夏

a steamy night
  dense with honeysuckle—
sleep eludes

fog shrouding
    a sheer pond and still boughs
silent dawn

comes with morning
    thru the dirt cragged, sundered —
a lily, burnt-orange

strident sandpipers
  foraging the ebb tide's rim —
shattering dawn

waves scalloping
over lost dugout canoes —

summer typhoon

the sky lightens
    as a sudden shower pauses —
rain droplets from the elms

black-winged seagulls
    skimming emerald waves —
seeking forenoon fare

nimbus clouds
    after a lashing summer squall
pass on

a wooden cask brims
with water from a bamboo trough—
crepe myrtle redden

cornstalks furrow —
fallen apples ferment —
indian summer daze

fall tempest

across a parched chaparral

tumbleweeds

fallen grapes fermenting
honey bees
spinning on their backs

gentle winds
    fanning vermillion feathers—
flamingoes settle
their hue deepening
as day closes

cloud hazy night
   an orange moon haunting
all souls' feast

Japanese lanterns light
a maine harvest —
moonless long night

humid night
rain puddles glowing
with a bright moon

clear dusk ~
    after a rainshower
fireflies winking

twilight winds toting
       morning glory scents —
the crickets singing

a bush-shrike whistling
     from a hackberry nest —
dusk echoes

a harsh cry —
    wading sandhill cranes
take flight

New Year's dawn
   okāsan tending the hearth—
young water, green tea

rice-cake flowers —
    a thousand paper cranes —
New Year's morning

snow-dusted field
two handfuls of crumbs
sparrows swarming

north winds
    drifting snow to the gate
darkest cold night

moonlit sleet
        glazing a wren's nest
winter keeps

snowdrifts crest
whitetail deer meandering pathless —
deep storm

prowling the tundra
    winter's wild calling
a lone wolf

darkness gathers
outside this silent gate —
I pass unseen

rain carved mud
gives up broken fossils
timeworn shadows

an oaken bucket
   cast into a burnt-brick well
echoing

tomodachi
warmheartedly we part
knowing our concord shall span
endless seasons

Artist & Author

The compilers of this chapbook are natives of Minnesota, currently residing on a small farm with their three sons in Semmes, Mobile County, Alabama.

The artist, **Mary E. Rodning,** was graduated from Gustavus Adolphus College (B.A., *cum laude,* Biology) and the University of Rochester (M.A., Biology/Science Education). She has studied Norwegian folk painting with Mr. Jon Gunderson, Minneapolis, Minnesota. Her interest in the *sumi-e* style of Oriental watercolor/brush painting was kindled while residing in Okinawa, Japan, and while under the tutelage of a Japanese-style painter, Ms. Hiede Haakenson. During 1984 she received certification for completion of a graduate course entitled "Chinese Landscape and Watercolor Painting" at the Zhejiang Academy of Fine Arts, Hangzhou, People's Republic of China (sponsored by the Division of

Continuing Education and Extension, Duluth Center, University of Minnesota), directed by Lu Yan-Shao, Chinese master painter. She has recently commenced a study of calligraphy with Japanese Master Takyu of the Seiun Kai, with the assistance of Ms. Takeko Cartwright and Yoshiko Britain. She is a member of the *Sumi-e Society of America, Ikebana International* (Mobile Chapter), *Friends of the Origami Center of America, Mobile Art Association,* and *Alabama State Poetry Society.* She is an art instructor at the *Fine Arts Museum of the South* in Mobile.

The author, **Charles B. Rodning,** was graduated from Gustavus Adoplhus College (B.S., *magna cum laude,* Biology, Chemistry), the University of Rochester School of Medicine and Dentistry (M.D.), and the University of Minnesota Health Sciences Center (Ph.D., Anatomy). His interest in Oriental poetry was revived and deepened while residing in Okinawa, Japan. He is currently Associate Professor, Departments of Surgery and Anatomy, College of Medicine, University of South Alabama, Mobile, Alabama; Fellow, International College of Surgeons; and Fellow, American College of Surgeons. He is a member of the *Sumi-e Society of America* and *Alabama State Poetry Society*. Several of his poems have been published in poetry periodicals, including *Orphic Lute, Piedmont Literary Review, American Poetry Anthology, National Poetry Anthology, Poets At Work, Tightrope, Bird Verse Portfolio, The Red Pagoda, Daring Poetry Quarterly, Odessa Poetry Review, Parnassus Literary Review, Modern Haiku, Dragonfly, Frogpond, Hieroglyphics,* and *Proof Rock.* He is also a recent prizewinner in the American Poetry Contest.

Finis